SNAPSHOTS IN HISTORY

PEARL HARBOR

Day of Infamy

by Stephanie Fitzgerald

PEARL HARBOR

Day of Infamy

by Stephanie Fitzgerald

Content Adviser: Derek Shouba, Adjunct History Professor
and Assistant Provost, Roosevelt University

Reading Adviser: Susan Kesselring, M.A., Literacy Educator,
Rosemount–Apple Valley–Eagan (Minnesota) School District

COMPASS POINT BOOKS
MINNEAPOLIS, MINNESOTA

✦ COMPASS POINT BOOKS

151 Good Counsel Drive
P.O. Box 669
Mankato, MN 56002-0669

Visit Compass Point Books on the Internet at
www.compasspointbooks.com
or e-mail your request to
custserv@compasspointbooks.com

For Compass Point Books
Jennifer VanVoorst, Jaime Martens, XNR Productions, Inc.,
Catherine Neitge, Keith Griffin, and Carol Jones

Produced by White-Thomson Publishing Ltd.
Tel.: 0044 (0)1273 403990
210 High Street, Lewes BN7 2NH

For White-Thomson Publishing
Stephen White-Thomson, Brian Krumm, Amy Sparks, Tinstar Design Ltd.
www.tinstar.co.uk, Derek Shouba, Joselito F. Seldera, Bill Hurd,
and Timothy Griffin

Library of Congress Cataloging-in-Publication Data
Fitzgerald, Stephanie.

Pearl Harbor : day of infamy / by Stephanie Fitzgerald.
p. cm. — (Snapshots in history)
Includes bibliographical references and index.
ISBN-13: 978-0-7565-1622-2 (hardcover)
ISBN-10: 0-7565-1622-6 (hardcover)
ISBN-13: 978-0-7565-1822-6 (paperback)
ISBN-10: 0-7565-1822-9 (paperback)
1. Pearl Harbor (Hawaii), Attack on, 1941—Juvenile literature.
I. Title. II. Series.
D767.92.F57 2005
940.54'26693—dc22   2005027148

CONTENTS

Day of Infamy

December 7, 1941, marks one of the darkest days in United States history. In what seemed like the blink of an eye, more than 2,000 Americans lay dead and the pride of the United States Navy was reduced to a smoking wreck. The Japanese military had struck the United States while it slept and driven a spike directly through its heart.

For the men and women stationed at Pearl Harbor in Oahu in 1941, life was good. They knew war was coming, but for the moment these young recruits were living in paradise. Oahu is one of the Hawaiian Islands, located in the Pacific Ocean. With its beautiful beaches and blue, sunny skies, Oahu is a popular vacation spot. Many of the young men and women who were stationed there had never

Fires raged aboard the USS West Virginia after Japanese pilots bombed the ship.

been away from their homes before. Most had never been anywhere as beautiful as Oahu.

During the week, sailors took to the sea on giant battleships, practicing maneuvers and taking target practice. Pilots flew through the skies, perfecting their aim with the planes' guns and practicing dropping bombs. The nurses in the hospital ward treated patients whose complaints were rarely worse than a bad case of sunburn.

Weekends were for relaxing. On Saturday night, there was always a battle of the ships' bands, a dance to attend, or a movie to see. Sundays were for sleeping late, attending church in the morning, and playing baseball or golf in the afternoon. For everyone stationed at Pearl Harbor, December 7 should have been just like any other Sunday. Instead, it became a waking nightmare, filled with terror, fire, suffering, and death.

At 7:55 that morning, many of the troops stationed at Pearl Harbor were still in bed. Others were just finishing breakfast. When the sound of planes overhead first reached their ears, most people thought they were U.S. Army planes. Even when the first bomb fell, many figured the pilots were taking target practice.

Within seconds, any sense of well-being on the island of Oahu was destroyed. That buzz in the air was the sound of hundreds of Japanese planes. Their pilots were intent on destroying every last plane, ship, building, and person at the Pearl Harbor base.

As bombs rocked the mighty ships moored on Battleship Row, sailors were thrown from their bunks or blown off the decks into the water. Great holes were ripped in the ships' hulls, sending water rushing into the men's quarters. As sailors closed and locked waterproof doors to keep the water out, they realized that they were sealing their own doom. They were trapping themselves inside ships that were raging with fire and beginning to sink.

The USS Arizona *burned as puffs of smoke from anti-aircraft guns filled the sky.*

Within moments, all of the ships on Battleship Row had been hit with torpedoes or bombs. The harbor's waters were slick with oil. Fires raged everywhere out of control, and thick, black smoke filled the sky. Sailors who were not immediately killed by explosions were burned by the fires that the explosions started. Others who made it into the water found it impossible to swim. The weight of their uniforms dragged them down, and the oil made their skin so slippery that it was hard to pull them from the water.

American planes were like sitting ducks when the attack occurred. Almost every plane on the ground was destroyed or damaged that day.

At the same time, Japanese bombers were attacking the airfields scattered across the island. The American planes were lined up wingtip to wingtip, like cars in a parking lot. Their pilots were eating breakfast. The ammunition for their guns—and the anti-aircraft guns on the ground—was under lock and key. Within minutes, nothing remained of the planes but flaming wrecks. Pilots' barracks, fire stations, and fire trucks were destroyed.

"A SLEEPING GIANT"

According to legend, Japanese Admiral Isoroku Yamamoto said the Japanese attack had awakened "a sleeping giant." People often mention this quotation in studies of Pearl Harbor. Though it makes for a good story, there is no evidence that Yamamoto really said that.

The attack ended less than two hours after it began. Twenty-one ships were sunk or damaged, 188 aircraft were destroyed, and 159 aircraft were damaged. Most of these aircraft were hit before they even had a chance to take off. American dead equaled 2,403, including 68 civilians. There were 1,178 military personnel and civilians wounded.

Japan's sneak attack on the United States was a huge military victory. It would enable the Japanese to dominate the war in the Pacific for at least six months while the U.S. Navy rebuilt and repaired its fleet. But it was also a major political mistake. The Japanese attack had awakened a sleeping giant. It would spur the American people to complete support for a war with Japan. Within four years, absolute victory would belong to the United States and its allies. ◣

The Road to War

The relationship between Japan and the United States had become strained as early as 1931—10 years before the attack on Pearl Harbor. That year, Japan invaded Manchuria, a part of China. Many other countries, including Great Britain and the United States, had colonial interests around the world, but they did not like the idea of Japan expanding its empire.

In 1937, Japan began its attempt to take over all of China. In response, the United States increased the military and financial aid they had already been providing to the Chinese. The United States also increased its military power in the Pacific and cut off the shipment of oil and other raw materials to Japan.

Japan was a small nation that did not have many natural resources. The government

The Japanese army entered Nanking, China, in 1938, killing women and children as they went. These actions further soured relations with the United States.

especially wanted to get nickel, iron, tin, oil, and rubber—all materials that were necessary for war—from other countries. Now that the United States was not supplying them with these types of raw materials, Japanese leaders saw Southeast Asia, which was rich in natural resources, as a "Southern Resources Area."

JAPAN'S AGGRESSION

The U.S. government was alarmed by Japanese aggression in Southeast Asia for more than political reasons. During the invasion of China, the Japanese Imperial Army tortured and brutally murdered more than 250,000 men, women, and children in the Nanking region alone.

The United States had its own interests in Southeast Asia, including territories in the Philippines, Samoa, Guam, Wake Island, and Hawaii. American leaders did not want Japan to overrun the area and threaten U.S. possessions. They were also concerned that Japan would keep them from doing business with the Chinese.

Japanese leaders wanted access to Southeast Asia's resources and markets, and they were willing to do anything to get them. Chinese and British troops in Southeast Asia represented roadblocks to the Japanese plan to conquer the area. But the Japanese government saw the U.S. Pacific Fleet stationed at Pearl Harbor as the only thing that was really standing in the way.

On September 27, 1940, Japan signed the Tripartite Pact with Germany and Italy to form the Axis Alliance. By signing this pact, the three countries were agreeing to help each other with military, economic, and political needs. That same year, Japanese troops invaded French Indochina, a federation of French colonies and territories in Southeast Asia. This area today makes up the countries of Vietnam, Laos, and Cambodia. Japan was moving forward with its plans in Southeast Asia even though its leaders knew that, in the end, it would mean war with the United States.

German troops invaded countries in Europe even before Japan signed the Tripartite Pact with Germany and Italy. The German army met little resistance as it rolled through the streets of Prague, then in the country of Czechoslovakia, in 1939.

17

In August 1941, four months before the Pearl Harbor attack, U.S. President Franklin D. Roosevelt (left) met with Prime Minister of Great Britain Winston Churchill to discuss the war effort.

Meanwhile, war was raging in Europe. Japan's allies—Germany and Italy—were fighting with Great Britain and would soon invade Russia. The Germans were rolling through Europe, taking over everything in their path. Though many countries tried to stop the invading forces, it seemed as if Great Britain was the only nation capable of holding them off. The British were taking a hard beating, though, and were hoping for help from their longtime ally, the United States.

The United States had been sending war materials to Great Britain to help fight the Axis Alliance. When Great Britain was unable to pay for these materials, U.S. President Franklin Delano Roosevelt came up with the Lend-Lease Act. This act enabled the United States to simply transfer, rather than sell, war materials to its allies. By the end of the war, the United States would provide about $50 billion in aid to more than 40 countries. It was up to the president to decide how each country would pay the United States back. Most, however, never had to. But as much as President Roosevelt tried to help America's allies in Europe and Southeast Asia, he knew the American people would not agree to fight in this war.

No matter what was going on in Europe and the Pacific, most American citizens were determined not to enter the war. Most Americans were isolationists. They did not want to get involved in a war that they felt did not concern them at all. By the end of 1941, however, all of that would change.

By early 1941, the Japanese government had realized that they either had to try to make peace with the United States or prepare for war. Government leaders tried to do both. Peace talks between the two nations began in February of that year, but officials on both sides found it very difficult to agree on anything. The United States wanted Japan to stop taking over other Asian nations. Japan, of course, did not want to comply. ◣

Friend or Foe?

As peace talks were being held in 1941, Japanese military leaders were also putting together a plan for war. Not all Japanese leaders wanted to start a war with the United States. But on October 16, 1941, Hideki Tojo, who had been the war minister, was made premier of Japan. This was a very powerful position. Tojo had always supported the idea of a war with the United States. Now he had the power to make it happen.

The plan revolved around the base at Hawaii's Pearl Harbor, which had been home to the U.S. Pacific Fleet since the spring of 1940. Its size and shape made Pearl Harbor one of the largest and best-sheltered harbors in the Pacific Ocean.

With 10 square miles (26 square kilometers) of navigable water, the harbor is deep enough for

Saburo Kurusu, a special representative from Japan, visited the United States in November 1941. He was supposedly carrying the Japanese government's terms for a peaceful settlement of Japanese-American relations in the Pacific.

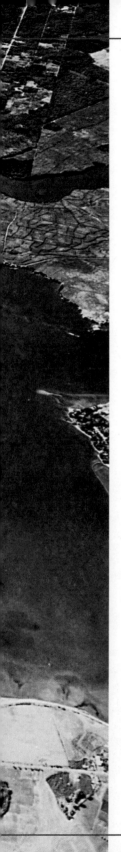

ships to sail in, but—luckily for the United States—it is also a bit shallow. The Navy had probably not considered this point when selecting Pearl Harbor as a base of operations, but the benefits became very clear right after the attack. Ships that were sunk in the harbor could be raised from the bottom. If they had been sunk in deep water, they would have been lost forever.

The entrance to Pearl Harbor is narrow, so it could be guarded easily. In 1941, one side of the entrance was protected by coral reefs, and the other side was protected by forts. There was also an anti-torpedo and boat net that stretched across the entrance. The net was moved aside when U.S. ships exited and entered the harbor. But it was put back immediately after the ships passed through. With this system in place, it would be almost impossible for an enemy ship to get into the harbor. Finally, the Naval Base at Pearl Harbor was so big that the entire U.S. Navy could dock, get fuel and supplies, and be repaired all at once, in one place.

Pearl Harbor was calm and orderly
before the December 7 attack.

23

In the center of the harbor is Ford Island, home to the Naval Air Station and patrol and utility plane hangars. Some of the deepest waters in Pearl Harbor are right off Ford Island, so battleships were moored there. That area, called Battleship Row, is where the USS *California*, USS *Maryland*, USS *Oklahoma*, USS *Tennessee*, USS *West Virginia*, USS *Arizona*, and USS *Nevada* were positioned when the Japanese attacked.

To the southeast of Ford Island were the Naval Station, the hospital, and Hickam Field Army Air Base. The Ewa Field Air Base was across the entrance from Hickam, and a third airfield, Wheeler, was north of Pearl Harbor in the center of Oahu.

The idea to attack Pearl Harbor came from Admiral Isoroku Yamamoto, who was commander of the Japanese Fleet. Yamamoto had gone to school in the United States and had later been a representative of the Japanese Navy in Washington, D.C. He had seen the strength of American industry with his own eyes, and he knew that now those energies were focused on providing arms for U.S. military forces.

Yamamoto believed that the only way the Japanese military could cripple the U.S. Fleet was with a surprise attack. But he also realized the attack would only put the U.S. Navy out of commission for a while. Even though he had masterminded the plan to attack Pearl Harbor, Yamamoto was worried about what would happen after the attack. He did not believe his country

would win a long war with the United States. He told a member of the Japanese cabinet:

Admiral Isoroku Yamamoto was the mastermind behind the Pearl Harbor attack.

In the first six to twelve months of a war with the United States and Great Britain I will run wild and win victory upon victory. But then, if the war continues after that, I have no expectation of success.

25

Despite Yamamoto's fears, in the spring of 1941 the crews on Japanese aircraft carriers began training for the special tactics they would need in the Pearl Harbor attack.

They practiced refueling their ships at sea—something that had never been done before—and taking off from aircraft carriers in rough waters.

In October 1941, the Japanese naval general staff gave their final approval to Yamamoto's plan. The navy would form a special task force that would be commanded by Vice Admiral Chuichi Nagumo. The strike force was made up of six aircraft carriers that would be accompanied by more than 20 supporting vessels. A separate group of submarines was sent along as well to sink any American warships that escaped the harbor.

The day selected for the attack, which the Japanese called "X-Day," was December 8 in Japan—December 7 in Hawaii. Japanese military leaders chose that date because it was a Sunday. They knew that all of the U.S. Navy ships would be at anchor and that most of the sailors, pilots, and Marines would be enjoying the morning off.

The plan depended on complete surprise. If the United States found out about the attack, the Japanese would have little hope of success. Japanese naval high command could call back Nagumo's strike force up until December 6. After that, it would be up to the strike force leader to decide whether or not to continue on with the attack. If a U.S. patrol boat spotted the strike

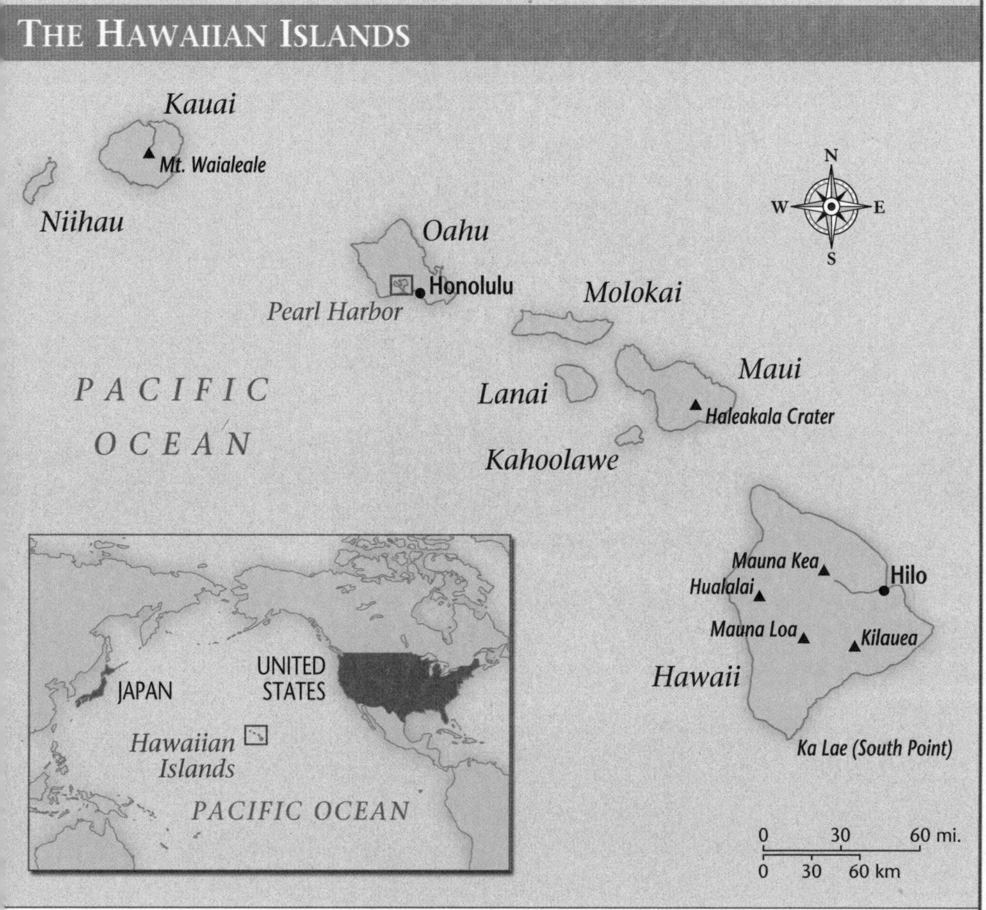

THE HAWAIIAN ISLANDS

Kauai

▲ Mt. Waialeale

Niihau

Oahu

● Honolulu

Pearl Harbor

Molokai

PACIFIC

Lanai

Maui

▲ Haleakala Crater

OCEAN

Kahoolawe

Mauna Kea ▲

Hualalai ▲

● Hilo

Mauna Loa ▲

▲ Kilauea

JAPAN

UNITED
STATES

Hawaii

Hawaiian ☐
Islands

Ka Lae (South Point)

PACIFIC OCEAN

| 0 | 30 | 60 mi. |
| 0 | 30 | 60 km |

force on the day before X-Day and the element of surprise was lost, Nagumo could make the decision to call off the attack.

Nagumo's fleet gathered in Tankan Bay in the Kurile Islands and set sail for Hawaii on November 26. To avoid being seen, they used a North Pacific route that nobody used in the winter because the weather was so bad. The seas were rough and there was often fog. The strike force had to maintain complete silence even in the dark.

Pearl Harbor was the most important U.S. military base in the Pacific region.

27

Row upon row of Japanese Zeros took off from the deck of the HJMS Shokaku.

They couldn't use their radios to talk to each other. The only way people on different ships could communicate with each other was with flashes of light or with flags.

28

Meanwhile, peace talks continued in Washington, D.C. On December 1, Japanese leaders decided that they could not accept the peace terms proposed by the United States. The decision to attack Pearl Harbor was made. But Japan did not declare war on the United States. American leaders were not told that the Japanese had decided to end negotiations. They were led to believe that the peace talks would continue.

On December 2, Admiral Yamamoto radioed the message to the strike force:

> *Climb Mount Niitaka 1208.*

That was the code for "proceed with attack," scheduled for midnight on December 8, Japanese time. By dawn on December 7, Hawaii time, the task force had traveled to within a little more than 200 miles (322 km) north of Oahu without being spotted by U.S. forces.

SURPRISE OR WARNING?

On December 1, the Emperor of Japan gave his approval of the plan to attack Pearl Harbor. Admiral Yamamoto wanted to give the United States a warning, but Japan's Premier Hideki Tojo fought for and won the right to mount a surprise attack. But Tojo did agree to compromise a little: U.S. Secretary of State Cordell Hull would be notified at 1 P.M. Washington, D.C., time on December 7 that Japan was breaking off peace talks. At 1 P.M. in Washington it would be 7:30 A.M. in Hawaii. That was just 30 minutes before the attack on Pearl Harbor and too late for the U.S. military to take useful action.

Warning Signs

Some people think that U.S. government leaders knew that the Japanese were going to attack Pearl Harbor. Looking back, it seems as if there were many clear warning signs. They think that President Roosevelt wanted the attack to happen so that Americans would agree with his belief that the United States had to join the war. However, most historians do not agree with the claim that Roosevelt purposely did not take any action to avoid the attack. We can look back now and see the warning signs, but at the time these signals were either misunderstood or just came too late to help.

By 1941, the U.S. military had broken the secret code that Japanese leaders used to communicate their plans and ideas. There were also U.S. ambassadors living and working around the world. They often heard stories from

Some members of President Roosevelt's Cabinet suspected that Japanese forces would attack the United States.

other diplomats that they passed onto American leaders in Washington, D.C. There was very little that the Japanese were talking about that the United States did not know of.

At the beginning of the year, U.S. Secretary of the Navy Frank Knox wrote to the Secretary of War Henry L. Stimson with a warning—and an opinion—that would prove to be correct:

> *If war eventuates with Japan, it is believed easily possible that hostilities would be initiated by a surprise attack upon the Fleet or the Naval Base at Pearl Harbor.*

It makes sense, then, that in November, as peace talks were breaking down, the U.S. Navy Department was expecting trouble. Unfortunately, they were completely wrong about how or where this trouble would start. They sent warnings to their bases in the Philippines and on Guam that a Japanese attack was possible. That made the most sense, because the Philippine Islands are relatively close to Japan. Defenses in both areas had been strengthened. Submarines had been stationed around other military bases in the Pacific, including Wake and Midway islands, for protection.

But because Hawaii was so far away from Japan, the United States focused on preventing sabotage by Japanese citizens living on the islands. Sabotage was a valid concern. There were definitely spies passing information about the Pearl Harbor base back to their leaders in Japan.

In an attempt to protect their aircraft from sabotage, military leaders gathered together all of the planes at each of Pearl Harbor's airfields.

SPY IN HAWAII

Takeo Yoshikawa was a Japanese spy living on the island of Oahu. His job was to count the American warships in Pearl Harbor and note their locations. He then reported this information to his superiors in Japan. His last report before the attack was made on December 6. After the Pearl Harbor attack, the U.S. government forced more than 100,000 Japanese-Americans living on the West Coast to move into relocation camps. They were mistakenly accused of being loyal to Japan. In reality, there were probably very few Japanese spies or loyalists living in the United States.

Admiral Husband Kimmel was the commander of the Pacific Fleet at Pearl Harbor in 1941.

They were lined up, wingtip to wingtip, so that they could be easily guarded. That strategy turned out to be a fatal mistake.

Just 10 days before the attack, Commander of the Pacific Fleet Admiral Husband Kimmel received a strong message from the Navy Department. It read in part:

> *This dispatch is to be considered a war warning. Negotiations with Japan ... have ceased and an aggressive move by Japan is expected within the next few days.*

The message listed the Philippines, Thailand, and Borneo as possible targets, but not Hawaii.

33

Even the people who sensed that a war was coming never thought that the first shots would be fired on Hawaii. Nobody thought that Japanese ships could carry enough fuel to sail to Hawaii and back. At 3,850 miles (6,196 km) away, it was just too far. Likewise, no one thought that a large strike force would be able to sail all the way from Japan to Hawaii without being discovered. They also thought Pearl Harbor was too well defended for an outside attack. They had no way of knowing how wrong they were.

Amazingly, there were even more concrete warnings on the day of the attack. In the hours before dawn, the U.S. destroyer *Ward* and two minesweepers, *Condor* and *Crossbill*, were patrolling the entrance to Pearl Harbor. While scanning the water, R.C. McCloy, *Condor's* officer on deck, saw what he thought was a submarine periscope. A report was quickly sent to the *Ward*. The men woke up their skipper, Lieutenant William W. Outerbridge, who searched the area for about an hour. The periscope was no longer in sight. At 4:35 A.M. Outerbridge sent his men who were not on duty back to their bunks. Because they could not confirm whether McCloy had really seen a submarine periscope, no one on any of the ships reported the incident.

Two hours later, a lookout woke Outerbridge again. This time there was no doubt that a small sub was just 50 yards (46 meters) away. The *Ward* attacked the sub with gunfire and depth charges, eventually sinking the vessel.

At 6:53 A.M., Outerbridge reported to Pearl Harbor:

> *We have attacked, fired upon, and dropped depth charges upon [a] submarine operating in defensive sea area.*

Lieutenant Commander Harold Kaminsky, the radio officer on watch at Pearl Harbor, received the message and tried to pass it along. Unfortunately Kaminsky had trouble reaching his superior officers.

A Japanese two-man submarine that tried to attack a ship in Pearl Harbor was sunk with shells and depth charges.

35

The first officer that Kaminsky was finally able to reach thought the report was false. There had been several false alarms reported that day. But Kaminsky, who did not think it was a false alarm, refused to give up. He then contacted the staff duty officer, who finally reached Admiral Husband Kimmel at about 7:40 A.M. Not realizing an attack was just about to happen, Kimmel decided to wait to make sure the report was right before doing anything. Incredibly, despite the fact that an enemy sub was spotted and sunk outside of its entrance, Pearl Harbor was not put on alert.

At 6:15 A.M., about 200 miles (322 km) north of Pearl Harbor, the 183 Japanese planes in the first attack wave took off from their carriers. At the time, Privates Joseph L. Lockard and George E. Elliot were operating a mobile radar unit near the northern tip of Oahu. They were supposed to shut down at 7 A.M., but Elliot wanted to practice. Radar was a new invention at the time, and the private was eager to learn more about it.

How Radar Works

A transmitter sends out a strong radio wave and a receiver listens for when that wave hits something, creating an echo. When that echo bounces back to the receiver, it shows that there is something out there, as well as how far away that object is.

At 7:02 A.M., Lockard and Elliot saw a large blip approaching Oahu from the north. To their eyes, this blip represented at least 50 planes. The men quickly called Lieutenant Kermit Tyler at the Fort Shafter Information Center near the harbor to report the sighting.

Soldiers used a new technology called radar to track a large group of planes heading toward Pearl Harbor. Radar rooms became commonplace aboard U.S. aircraft carriers.

As it turned out, a group of B-17 bombers coming from California was scheduled to arrive at the Pearl Harbor installation that day. They were on their way to help the U.S. forces that were in the Philippines.

37

Luckily for the United States, several U.S. aircraft carriers that were intended targets, including the USS Saratoga (foreground) and the USS Lexington, were not in Pearl Harbor at the time of the Japanese attack.

THE WARNING THAT CAME TOO LATE

General George C. Marshall had been made aware of a message sent from Tokyo to Japanese negotiators in Washington, D.C. The message had been discovered by U.S. codebreakers. It told the negotiators to break off peace talks with the United States. Marshall took this to mean that Japan might soon be attacking the United States. Marshall sent a message to Pearl Harbor, telling officers there to be on alert. His message reached the telegraph office in Honolulu at 7:33 A.M. on December 7. Unfortunately, it had not been marked "priority" and so was grouped with civilian mail. The message did not reach members of the Pearl Harbor command until 11:45 A.M. It was not decoded until 2:58 P.M., long after the Japanese attackers had done their damage.

Though the radar operators could see when something was heading toward them, they had no way to identify exactly what that "thing" was. There was no difference, on a radar screen, between enemy planes and friendly planes. Tyler assumed that the blip on the screen was the group of U.S. bombers. He told the soldiers to forget about it. Despite the order, Lockard and Elliot could not take their eyes off the group of planes. They followed the movement until 7:39 A.M., when it was lost in the echoes from the surrounding mountains.

Just minutes later, the first bombs would fall.

To! To! To!

The Japanese X-Day strike force was made up of six aircraft carriers—*Akagi, Hiryu, Kaga, Shokaku, Soryu,* and *Zuikaku*—which together carried more than 420 planes.

The carriers were supported by battleships, destroyers, and cruisers, as well as by tankers that could fuel the ships during their journey from Japan. When the assault group was about 200 miles (322 km) north of Oahu, the aircraft took off from their carriers.

Before they took off, the Japanese pilots prepared themselves for their mission. They all had a ceremonial breakfast of *sekhan*, which is a dish made of rice and beans, and Japanese wine called *sake*. Japanese people usually ate sekhan for special occasions, and this mission was a very special occasion.

Japanese dive-bombers prepared to take off in the early morning hours of December 7, 1941.

Every member of the Japanese strike force was ready to die during this attack. They were proud to give their lives for their country. As they waited for the start of their mission, many of the men prayed while others wrote letters to their families in case they did not make it back.

Finally, they each tied *hachimakis* (a sort of headband) around their heads. Written on each hachimaki was the word *hissho*, which meant "certain victory."

Mitsuo Fuchida was the air attack commander. He wore a special hachimaki. He also chose to wear red underwear and a red shirt. He knew that if he was wounded, the red clothing would hide the blood from his men. Then they could concentrate fully on their mission, rather than worrying about their leader.

At 5:30 A.M., two seaplanes flew off to scout the planned route to Oahu. The coast was clear. The Americans had no idea the Japanese were coming. Even though the time seemed right to start the attack, the pilots had to wait 20 minutes before they could take off. The weather was terrible and the sea was very rough. Taking off in those conditions would be too dangerous.

The first attack wave to leave the carriers was made up of 183 planes. There were torpedo bombers, dive-bombers, horizontal bombers, and fighter planes. The fighter planes took off first so that they could protect the torpedo planes and bombers. As soon as the first group of planes left each carrier deck, a second wave was brought up. In total, more than 350 Japanese planes left for the mission at Pearl Harbor.

Japanese pilots were given last-minute instructions before heading out to Pearl Harbor.

A Japanese aircraft carrier crew cheered the departing pilots. Japanese servicemen had high hopes for the Pearl Harbor attack.

As they were flying toward their targets, the pilots had to remain totally silent. The only way they could communicate with each other was by using hand signals. Commander Fuchida, who was leading the attack in a bomber, used the radio station that was broadcasting from Honolulu to check his course. As he zeroed in on the signal, he noticed that the station was playing music. That told him that the Americans had no idea an attack was coming.

ATTACK IN THE PHILIPPINES

The Japanese attacked other U.S. military installations on December 7, including the Philippines. The U.S. Far East Air Corps took heavy losses in that attack, losing almost 100 planes.

At 7:49 A.M., Fuchida had a radio operator send the signal "To! To! To!" (pronounced "toe, toe, toe") to his pilots. *To* is the first syllable of *totsugeki*—the Japanese word for "charge" or "attack." Minutes later the operator sent the message:

Tora, Tora, Tora!

This meant that complete surprise had been achieved. ◣

This Is Not a Drill!

Chapter

6

The attack on Pearl Harbor began at about 7:55 A.M. Hawaii time. Kukuichi Takahashi, who was leading the dive-bombers, dropped the first bomb on a seaplane ramp at the Pearl Harbor Naval Air Station on Ford Island. When people stationed at Pearl Harbor heard the planes approaching, many thought they were friendly planes. Even when the first bomb hit, many people thought the U.S. Army was taking target practice.

Rear Admiral William Furlong was standing on the deck of the *Oglala* when the first bomb fell. He knew something was seriously wrong when he saw the seaplane ramp explode into splinters. Then he got a close look at the bomber. The plane was flying so low that he could see the Japanese rising sun emblem on its wings.

U.S. seamen who witnessed the attack from a submarine base in Pearl Harbor could only watch in horror as the attack unfolded.

47

Lieutenant Commander Logan Ramsey, who was looking through the window of the Ford Island Command Center, also saw the first bomb explode. Without a moment's hesitation, he ran to the radio room and gave an order to the operators. They were to broadcast a message in all frequencies and in plain English:

Air raid. Pearl Harbor. This is NOT a drill!

At 7:58 A.M., the message went out to Pearl Harbor Commander Admiral Husband Kimmel, government officials in Washington, D.C., and to the headquarters of the U.S. Asiatic Fleet in the Philippines.

Furlong and Ramsey caught the first glimpses of the nightmare that was about to unfold. Imagine their horror if they had known the full scope of the disaster. At the exact moment that Japanese planes dropped their first bombs on the ships in the harbor's waters, other pilots were attacking the airfields.

The Japanese had come up with a perfect plan. They knew that if they attacked the airfields at the same time that they hit the harbor, the situation on the ground would be chaos. If they attacked the harbor first, American pilots might have been able to come to the ships' defenses. By attacking the airfields at the same time, though, they made sure that American planes would never have the chance to take off and challenge the Japanese pilots.

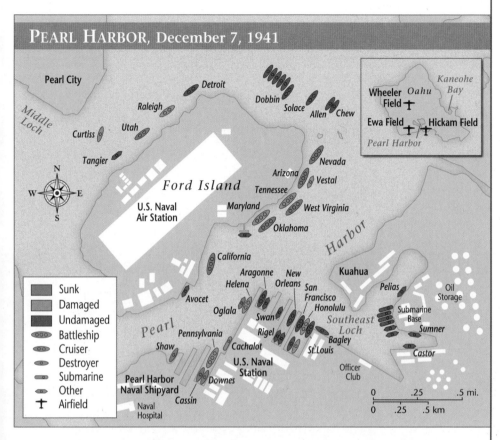

PEARL HARBOR, December 7, 1941

Pearl City
Detroit
Dobbin
Solace
Allen Chew
Raleigh
Utah
Curtiss
Tangier

Wheeler Oahu Kaneohe
Field + Bay
Ewa Field Hickam Field
+ +
Pearl Harbor

Ford Island

Nevada
Arizona Vestal
Tennessee
U.S. Naval Maryland West Virginia
Air Station
Oklahoma

Harbor

California
Aragonne New Kuahua
Helena Orleans San
Avocet Francisco Pelias Oil
Oglala Honolulu Storage
Swan Submarine
Pearl Pennsylvania Rigel Southeast Base Sumner
Shaw Bagley
Cachalot Loch
Downes St.Louis Castor
U.S. Naval
Pearl Harbor Station Officer
Naval Shipyard Club
Cassin
Naval
Hospital

Legend:
- Sunk
- Damaged
- Undamaged
- Battleship
- Cruiser
- Destroyer
- Submarine
- Other
- + Airfield

Middle Loch

N W E S

0 .25 .5 mi.
0 .25 .5 km

Because the planes had been clustered together for protection, there was little difficulty in destroying almost all of them.

The attack on Pearl Harbor destroyed and damaged ships and aircraft all over the island.

Kaneohe Bay Naval Station

The naval station at Kaneohe Bay, about 12 miles (20 km) northeast of Honolulu, was the first American military base to come under attack on that terrible morning of December 7. Within minutes, everything would be chaos. But when the first planes arrived, John Finn, the chief ordnance man at Kaneohe Bay, was still in bed. Finn was not alarmed when he heard the planes overhead. But the sharp, almost frantic knock at his door quickly put him on alert. The woman at the door told Finn he was needed at the hangar; then she turned and ran away.

Finn jumped into his car and raced to the hangar with Japanese fighter planes, called Zeros, roaring through the sky above him. When he reached the airstrip, Finn realized his options were limited. There were no anti-aircraft guns on the base. There were not even mounts for the machine guns.

It was time to improvise. Finn picked up a .30 caliber machine gun, loads of ammunition, and dragged it all about 20 yards (18 m) out onto the runway. From that spot, he spent the next two hours shooting at Japanese planes. He didn't even seem to notice the bullets and shrapnel flying around him, even though he was hit more than 20 times.

The Japanese pilots destroyed all but six of the 33 seaplane patrol boats at Kaneohe Bay, and they killed 18 men. Finn was credited with shooting down at least one Japanese plane. Almost a year later, he was awarded the Congressional Medal of Honor for his actions that day.

Hickam Field

Just moments after Kaneohe Bay was attacked, Japanese dive-bombers pounded the dozens of American planes that were parked at Hickam Field, located just southeast of Pearl Harbor. At the same time, Zeros began firing their machine guns up and down the rows of planes. Within minutes, the American aircraft were in flames.

No one at Hickam was ready for the attack. There was no ammunition in the planes. It was so early in the morning that the men were not even in uniform. But that did not stop them from trying to defend the airfield, sometimes with nothing more than a pistol. They ran from their barracks, pulling on clothes as they could, racing to get to the planes and get them in the air.

A group of B-17s flying from California ended up at Hickam Field during the attack. One pilot lost half his plane while trying to land.

Other men who had been servicing aircraft had no cover. They had no place to hide from the Japanese, but they refused to give up. As quickly as they could, some men ran to the aircraft and wrestled the machine guns out so that they could return fire. Others tried to get into their planes to fire the guns. But the Japanese were after more than planes. They wanted to destroy everything on the base, and kill the American pilots.

INCOMING B-17s

The B-17s that were coming in from California arrived at the airfields as the Japanese were attacking. The planes had been flying unarmed, so pilots could do little more than try to land when they reached Hickam. Unfortunately, they were taking fire from Japanese planes and from confused U.S. troops on the ground. Luckily, the bomber pilots managed to land their planes, many covered with bullet holes, across Oahu.

Zeros and dive-bombers attacked the pilots' barracks from every angle as men rushed out to reach their battle stations. Inside a dining hall, hundreds of men sat eating breakfast when a bomb crashed through the roof and exploded inside. Fire engines raced toward the burning planes—and became a favorite target of the Japanese pilots. All hope of saving the aircraft was lost.

Ewa Field

The Marine air station at Ewa Field, located 4 miles (6.4 km) west of Pearl Harbor, was taking heavy fire from Zeros launched from the aircraft carrier *Kaga*. The Marines had not had time to man their

anti-aircraft guns or even arm themselves with more than a sidearm or rifle. Despite the danger— and the uselessness of their actions—every man on the base ran into the firestorm to shoot back at their attackers.

Japanese pilots destroyed everything on the ground, including planes and hangars.

53

Japanese pilot Lieutenant Yoshio Shiga, the leader of this group of Zeros, was shocked by what he saw. He later talked about a Marine who stood without even noticing the machine gun bullets spraying the ground around him, emptying his pistol at Shiga's plane as it flew past. Shiga noted the man's bravery in his battle

ANTI-AIRCRAFT GUNS

An anti-aircraft gun is a weapon, usually a large caliber machine gun or a cannon, that is used on the ground to fire on airborne craft. These weapons are often mounted on stands that can rotate to "chase" after planes.

report and later described him as the bravest American he had ever seen.

Although every pilot at Ewa tried to get his plane in the air, most planes were either burning or covered with too many bullet holes to fly. Meanwhile, a second group of Zeros descended on Ewa. It seemed the Marines' nightmare would never end. Six additional Japanese fighters now joined in firing on the Marine base. When the dust finally settled, Japanese pilots were responsible for the destruction of all 47 planes on the ground.

Japanese pilots flew planes called Zeros in the attacks at Ewa Field and the other airfields. They were called Zeros by the Japanese Navy because they were Type 0 carrier fighters.

Wheeler Field

The Japanese pilots also targeted U.S. soldiers' barracks in their attacks on the airfields.

During the first wave of the attack, dive-bombers dropped about 35 bombs on the hangars at Wheeler Field, located in the middle of the island

of Oahu. Luckily, the smoke from burning planes hid some of the planes on the ground, so they were not hit. The men quickly moved the planes away from the fire and prepared to arm them.

At the time, aircraft were kept unarmed and the ammunition and guns were stored separately, mostly to prevent enemy sabotage. Now it was up to pilots to rescue the ammo from the burning hangars, arm their planes, and get them in the air. Four fighters from the 46th Pursuit Squadron were able get airborne before the second Japanese wave arrived and started shooting at the planes and men on the airfield.

Meanwhile, George Welch and Kenneth Taylor, both second lieutenants, had been jolted awake by the scream of low-flying planes and the bone-jarring sound of exploding bombs. The men had only graduated from pilot training school a year before and were hardly prepared to fight a war.

Their lack of experience did not stop the young pilots, though. Taylor quickly made a call to the grass landing and takeoff strip at Haleiwa, near Wheeler Field, where the 47th Pursuit Squadron had been sent for target practice. He instructed the crew to get two P-40 planes fueled up and ready for combat.

Even though they did not have permission from their commanding officers, Welch and Taylor raced to the airfield and took off in their planes. They were just two of about 20 brave American pilots that made it off the ground that day.

Armed only with small .30 caliber guns, the pilots found a group of Japanese dive-bombers near the Marine airfield at Ewa and attacked them. Welch and Taylor each shot down one dive-bomber before Welch was hit. As they returned to the Pearl Harbor area, they each downed another bomber.

Running low on ammunition, the pilots landed at Wheeler Field to rearm. As Welch and Taylor were getting ready to take off, a wave of enemy bombers escorted by Zeros swarmed toward the field. The men flew right into the enemy's formation where Welch shot a Zero that was on Taylor's tail. As he was covering Taylor, Welch was

Some Japanese bombers were shot down during the attack.

hit again, but quickly struck back, shooting down another attacking plane.

At that point, the men returned once again to Haleiwa to rearm. By the time they got airborne again, the Japanese attack force had departed. By 9:45 A.M., the attack at Wheeler Field had left 83 aircraft destroyed, 38 enlisted men dead, and 59 wounded.

FRIENDLY FIRE

During the attacks, very few U.S. planes were able to take off to try to defend Pearl Harbor. To make matters worse, in the chaos and confusion of the day, about a dozen American planes were shot down by "friendly fire" from their own troops.

Nightmare on Battleship Row

More than 90 ships lay at anchor at Pearl Harbor at the time of the attack. In a rare stroke of luck on this horrible day, U.S. aircraft carriers were away from the harbor. The *Enterprise* had been sent to carry fighter planes to Wake Island. The *Lexington* was transporting bombers to Midway Island. The *Saratoga* had just finished being repaired on the West Coast and was set to return to Pearl Harbor, and the *Yorktown* was not yet combat ready.

Luckily, *Enterprise* and several other ships were delayed in returning to Pearl Harbor because of bad weather. That bit of good fortune might have saved the United States from final defeat in World War II. For the first time in history, aircraft carriers would play a huge role in combat—especially in the Pacific arena.

The Japanese attack on Pearl Harbor crippled the U.S. Fleet.

Just before 8 A.M., Japanese bombers fanned out over Pearl Harbor. Since the aircraft carriers were not present, the eight battleships became the Japanese pilots' primary targets. Seven battleships—the USS *Nevada*, USS *Arizona*, USS *West Virginia*, USS *Tennessee*, USS *Oklahoma*, USS *California*, and USS *Maryland*—were moored in Battleship Row. The USS *Pennsylvania* was in a nearby repair dock. Within the first few minutes of the attack, all of the battleships next to Ford Island had taken bomb or torpedo hits.

Some Japanese planes attacked from just 50 feet (15 m) in the air. They dropped torpedoes that traveled through the water and exploded when they hit a ship. Horizontal bombers dropped bombs from high in the air, where they would be out of reach of anti-aircraft guns. Dive-bombers flew high and then dove toward their target, dropped their bombs, and flew away.

CUSTOM TORPEDOES

Normally, torpedoes dropped from planes dive deep under water before straightening out and heading for their target. In Pearl Harbor, they would have hit bottom and exploded because the water is shallow. The Japanese developed a shallow water torpedo for this attack. They attached wooden fins to the torpedoes that kept the torpedoes level in the air from the time they were dropped. When the torpedo hit the water, the fins broke off and it was on its way to strike a target ship.

USS *Arizona*

In the seconds before the Japanese attacked, many sailors aboard the *Arizona* were finishing their breakfast. Some were talking about the fleet baseball championship that was to take place later in the afternoon. Others were still in their quarters sleeping. At the sound of the first explosions, the "general quarters" alarm was sounded, telling everyone to get to his battle station. Unfortunately, there would be a delay.

There was no way to salvage the badly damaged USS Arizona. Most of the men who were on board during the attack were trapped on the ship and died there.

63

Since it was Sunday, none of the ship's anti-aircraft guns were loaded, and the ammunition was under lock and key. One quick-thinking sailor, however, broke the padlock of an ammunition compartment and began handing out ammo.

Many crewmembers were now at their battle stations. But before they could start firing their anti-aircraft guns, a line of Japanese bombers roared over the *Arizona* and released their bombs. Five bombs crashed through the deck of the ship, and an armor-piercing bomb ignited the *Arizona's* forward ammunition magazine. There was a thundering explosion as all the ammunition that was stored there erupted into a giant ball of flame. The huge ship seemed to leap halfway out of the water before sinking like a stone into the mud.

USS VESTAL

The USS *Vestal*, which was moored next to the *Arizona*, had been hit by a bomb and was burning. When the *Arizona's* ammo storage exploded, though, an amazing thing happened—the blast saved the Vestal. The explosion sucked all of the oxygen from the area and, since fire cannot burn without oxygen, *Vestal's* fire was extinguished.

The explosion and the fires that followed killed 1,177 crewmen. It was the greatest single ship loss of the day and accounted for about half of the total lives lost on December 7.

The swiftness of the attack on the *Arizona* brought a quick end to that battle. But, as always happens in war, there was just enough time for individual acts of heroism. Early in the attack,

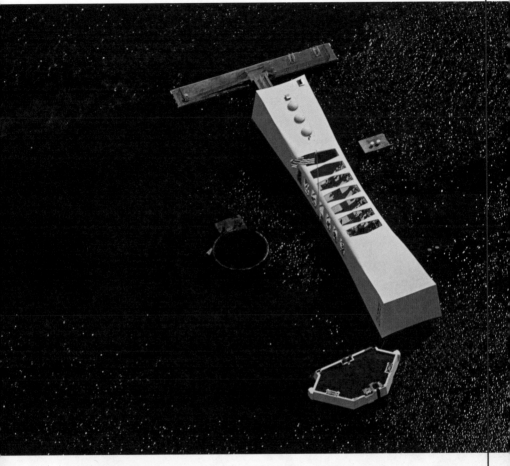

Lieutenant Commander Samuel G. Fuqua had been knocked unconscious by an explosion. But as soon as he came to, the brave officer directed firefighting and rescue efforts.

After the ship's forward magazine exploded, Fuqua was the *Arizona*'s senior surviving officer and was responsible for saving the ship's remaining crewmen. He organized human chains to get the sailors off the ship and stayed on board until the last man was removed. He was awarded the Medal of Honor for his heroism.

The USS Arizona *Memorial is located on the site where the ship sank in Pearl Harbor. A viewing platform and memorial spans the sunken ship.*

65

The USS Shaw *exploded after fire reached its ammunition stores.*

Major Alan Shapley was blown overboard in one of the explosions. His uniform was burned completely off his body. Soon after he went

overboard, he noticed another *Arizona* sailor, Earl Nightengale, who had also been thrown into the water. He was exhausted and covered in the oil that was pouring from the damaged ship. Nightengale soon found it too difficult to swim. Just when the sailor was certain he would drown, Major Shapley approached him and told him to hang on to his neck.

With Nightengale hanging onto his neck, Shapley began swimming toward shore. Soon he, too, was overcome by exhaustion. Nightengale told Shapley to leave him behind and save himself, but the major refused. Somehow, he managed to get himself and Nightengale to safety. For his bravery, Shapley was awarded the Silver Star Medal for heroism.

USS *Nevada*

Aboard the battleship *Nevada,* a band and a Marine guard stood at attention. As they did every Sunday morning, the Marines were getting ready to play "The Star-Spangled Banner" and raise the flag. But halfway through the national anthem, the rear gunner of a Japanese plane sprayed the ship with machine gun bullets. None of the sailors were hit, but bullets ripped into the ship's flag.

For just a moment, the band stopped playing— but just for a moment. The band picked up the anthem again as the Marine guard stood at attention and the sailors on deck stayed in ranks. It was not until the song was finished that the bandleader gave the "dismissed" order, and everyone on deck scrambled for cover.

About half an hour later, there was a brief lull in the attack. The USS *Nevada* was damaged, but the senior officer on the ship at the time, Lieutenant Commander Francis Thomas, managed to get the ship underway. He was going to try to move the ship toward open water. Before the *Nevada* could pull away, though, the lines mooring the ship to land had to be cut. Chief Boatswain Edwin J. Hill went over the side of the boat to cut the lines.

USS ENTERPRISE

At 6 A.M., as the USS *Enterprise* headed toward Pearl Harbor, some of the ship's planes were sent out to scout the area. As the planes approached the battle, they took fire from Japanese and American forces. Six of the *Enterprise*'s planes were shot down—at least one by "friendly fire."

The *Nevada* started moving immediately, so Hill couldn't climb back onboard. He did not want to be left behind, though, so he dove into the water and swam after his ship. Hill knew his shipmates were going into battle, and he wanted to fight beside them.

Hill made it back to his ship, but before the *Nevada* could clear the harbor entrance, the second wave of Japanese planes hit. The Japanese pilots concentrated their attack on the moving target. They hoped to sink the *Nevada* so that it would block the harbor entrance—and any hope of escape for the American ships. Lieutenant Commander Thomas and the men at the harbor control tower realized what the Japanese had in mind for the *Nevada*. The order was given to run the ship aground at Hospital Point. This quick thinking and decisive action kept the waterway clear.

By beaching the USS *Nevada, the harbor entrance was kept clear.*

USS *Oklahoma*

Meanwhile, a line of torpedo bombers was closing in on the battleship *Oklahoma*. In the early moments of the attack, there was no one manning the anti-aircraft guns. The Japanese pilots flew low and sped directly toward their target. Torpedoes dropped from the planes, splashed into the water, and darted toward the battleship where many of the crew members still slept.

Three torpedoes tore into the *Oklahoma*, creating explosions that rocked all of Battleship Row. Sailors poured onto the decks of the battleship, some still in their underwear, as they rushed to the anti-aircraft guns. But the ammunition was locked in steel compartments, and all of the firing locks had been removed from the anti-aircraft guns for

an admiral's inspection on Monday. The situation seemed hopeless.

As the *Oklahoma* was being bombed, the men were locking themselves into airtight compartments. They were trying to keep the water from filling up the whole ship. They were also hoping to wait for rescue in these dry rooms. But as the ship began to turn upside down and sink, they realized they were trapped.

One group of sailors realized that their only hope for escape was through a porthole. The biggest, strongest sailor was pushing the others through the tiny windowlike hatch as fast as he could. Once they all got out, he realized he was too big to fit through himself. This selfless sailor perished in his ship.

The USS Oklahoma (right) capsized, but the USS Maryland (left) was only slightly damaged.

After the second wave of attacks, Japanese Commander Fuchida looked over the damage. He saw that the repair docks and oil tanks were still standing and realized that they were important targets. He wanted to attack again, but Vice Admiral Nagumo was worried that the United States might be organizing a counterattack using the missing carriers.

Denying Fuchida's request was a major mistake. That decision spared repair shops and oil tanks, enabling the United States to quickly rebuild its ships and planes and join the fight in the Pacific. Still, when Fuchida and the rest of the Japanese planes returned to their aircraft carriers, they had reason to celebrate. Only 29 of the 350 planes involved in the attack had been lost. ◣

Black oil filled the harbor as the USS California, another ship badly damaged on Battleship Row, burned and began to sink.

Terror Under Water

Chapter

8

Though it must have seemed like days to the men on the ground, the last of the Japanese attackers was gone within two hours. But even after the attack ended, death and danger still threatened everyone in Pearl Harbor.

Badly burned men, covered in oil, were being pulled from the water and carried to makeshift hospitals. Doctors and nurses did their best to ease the sailors' pain while they waited for transport to fully functioning hospitals but there were many who never made it out of the water. As the fires burned through the day and night, hundreds of sailors were trapped underwater in their ships, praying for rescue. They banged on the inside of the metal ships, hoping to attract someone's attention. Throughout the night, the eerie sound of tapping could be heard throughout the harbor.

Water from fire hoses was no match for the fires that raged throughout the harbor.

Stephen B. Young was one such sailor. He was trapped in the number 4 turret of the *Oklahoma* with some of his crewmates. They were so certain they were going to die, that they placed a bet on how the end would come. Young said:

> *I'll bet you a dollar we suffocate before we drown.*

It seems they thought the only way to survive the horror of waiting for death was to joke about it. But there were three sailors who were not going to wait for anything. Seamen Mallaly, Weisman, and Roberts were going to try to swim up and out of the *Oklahoma*—something that seemed nearly impossible. The men would have to swim through the pitch-black, twisting and turning hallways of the ship and make it up three decks—a journey of 90 feet (27 m). Even if they could hold their breath that long, it was doubtful they would be able to find their way to the surface. Incredibly, the three sailors made it out and were able to lead rescuers to their crewmates trapped below.

AMERICAN LOSSES AT PEARL HARBOR	
2,403	*Americans killed, including 68 civilians*
1,178	*American soldiers and civilians wounded*
21	*ships of the U.S. Pacific Fleet sunk or damaged*
188	*aircraft destroyed*
159	*aircraft damaged*

About 25 hours after the sailors were originally trapped, sailors and engineers had gathered their equipment. They were ready to try cutting into the ship and locating the sailors inside. As the rescuers began cutting open the hull, water rushed into the compartment where the sailors were waiting. They were so close to rescue, but suddenly it was unclear whether they would be saved or drowned in the effort. This group of men was lucky. They were rescued. Unfortunately, there were more than 400 sailors still trapped elsewhere in the ship.

Battleship Row was obscured by heavy smoke rising from burning ships.

77

More than 1 million people visit the USS Arizona Memorial every year to pay their respects to Pearl Harbor's fallen sailors.

All through the harbor, sailors worked desperately to rescue their friends trapped in the sunken ships. Hundreds of men waited in water-filled, pitch-dark compartments while others

struggled to free them. The trapped men banged on walls to guide the rescuers. For days, sailors worked on deck and underwater, cutting through metal with torches until they could reach their shipmates.

But the men on the *Arizona* could not be saved. The ship's bottom lay in the mud, and its decks roared with flame. The fire was so hot that rescuers could not even get close to the ship. For the men who went down with their ship, the USS *Arizona* became their final resting place.

USS *ARIZONA*

The USS *Arizona* was too badly damaged to salvage. Much of the ruined ship still lies where it sank at the bottom of Pearl Harbor. Dedicated in 1962, the USS *Arizona* Memorial spans the mid-portion of the sunken ship. The open structure allows visitors to view the remains of the *Arizona* through the clear, shallow water. The memorial also lists the names of the *Arizona* sailors who were lost that day.

When the smoke cleared at Pearl Harbor, engineers worked to save the damaged ships. Because the water was so shallow, even sunken ships had a chance to sail again. One by one, the damaged ships were raised from the water, towed to dry dock, and repaired. Most of them would fight again. ◣

Rise of the Sleeping Giant

News of the attack at Pearl Harbor reached U.S. leaders in Washington, D.C., just minutes after it started. It was Sunday afternoon in the United States, and around the country people were enjoying a day of rest. Many were at home listening to a football game on the radio when the broadcast was interrupted with news of the attack.

The entire country was in shock—and deeply saddened by what they heard. But that shock would soon turn to anger and an unbreakable determination to defeat the Japanese at all costs. This was one outcome of the attack that the Japanese planners could not have entirely expected.

Although the attack seemed like a total success for the Japanese, it would turn into a disaster.

On December 8, 1941, President Franklin D. Roosevelt presented his "day of infamy" speech to the U.S. Congress and requested a declaration of war on Japan.

Many Japanese leaders, including Admiral Yamamoto, had warned that Japan would never beat the United States in a drawn-out war. Now, that war was a grim reality. Before Pearl Harbor, many Americans had been against going to war with anyone. After the attack, the nation was swept by a wave of patriotism. Americans felt they had no choice but to go to war. They had been attacked by surprise, and they were ready to fight back.

The day after the Pearl Harbor attack, thousands of young men lined up to join the armed forces.

When Prime Minister Winston Churchill of Great Britain heard that the United States would finally be joining the war effort, he was relieved. He wrote:

> *To have the United States at our side was to me the greatest joy. Now at this very moment I knew the United States was in the war, up to the neck and in to the death.*

After the Pearl Harbor attack, thousands of young men went to recruiting agencies to join. Sometimes the lines were several blocks long. Some men even waited in line overnight.

On December 8, President Roosevelt addressed the United States Congress and asked for a declaration of war. His speech was short, but it was powerful:

U.S. TROOPS JOIN WORLD WAR II

At the time of the Pearl Harbor attack, there were only 1.5 million soldiers in the U.S. armed forces. One million of them were still in training. Ultimately, 16 million Americans would serve in World War II.

> *Yesterday, December 7, 1941—a date which will live in infamy—the United States of America was suddenly and deliberately attacked by naval and air forces of the Empire of Japan.*
>
> *The United States was at peace with that nation and, at the solicitation of Japan, was still in conversation with its Government and its Emperor looking toward the maintenance of peace in the Pacific ...*

83

It will be recorded that the distance of Hawaii from Japan makes it obvious that the attack was deliberately planned many days or even weeks ago. During the intervening time the Japanese Government has deliberately sought to deceive the United States by false statements and expressions of hope for continued peace.

The attack yesterday on the Hawaiian Islands has caused severe damage to American naval and military forces. Very many American lives have been lost. In addition American ships have been reported torpedoed on the high seas between San Francisco and Honolulu.

Yesterday the Japanese Government also launched an attack against Malaya. Last night Japanese forces attacked Hong Kong. Last night Japanese forces attacked Guam. Last night Japanese forces attacked the Philippine Islands. Last night the Japanese attacked Wake Island. This morning the Japanese attacked Midway Island.

Japan has, therefore, undertaken a surprise offensive extending throughout the Pacific area. The facts of yesterday speak for themselves. The people of the United States have already formed their opinions and well understand the implications to the very life and safety of our nation. ... There is no blinking at the fact that our people, our territory, our interests are in grave danger.

> *I ask that the Congress declare that since the unprovoked and dastardly attack by Japan on Sunday, December seventh, a state of war has existed between the United States and the Japanese Empire.*

Japanese troops invaded and took over the U.S.-controlled island of Guam on December 10, 1941. Later in World War II, the island would be the scene of intense fighting between Japanese and American military forces.

The declaration of war that came that day would mark the beginning of a long and bloody struggle. Ultimately, more than 1 million Japanese and almost 300,000 American soldiers would lose their lives.

The Japanese had gained an advantage in the Pearl Harbor attack and dominated the war in the Pacific for the first six months. Once American troops and supplies were up and running again, though, the tide would turn. Allied victory would be complete in the Pacific and in Europe. As a satisfying bonus, Allied forces would ultimately destroy every Japanese ship that had been part of the Pearl Harbor attack. ◪

Timeline

September 18 1931

Japan invades Manchuria

September 27, 1940

Japan signs Tripartite Pact with Germany and Italy, forming the Axis Alliance

March 11, 1941

President Roosevelt approves the Lend-Lease Act

Spring 1941

Japanese crews start training for special tactics needed in Pearl Harbor attack

September 22, 1941

Japan invades French Indochina; the United States stops selling oil to Japan

October 1941

Japanese naval general staff gives final approval to Isoroku Yamamoto's plan; a special task force is created

October 16, 1941

War Minister Hideki Tojo is made premier of Japan

November 26, 1941

Japanese attack force leaves Tankan Bay and gets under way to Pearl Harbor

November 27, 1941

The U.S. War Department issues its "war warning" to American military bases in the Pacific

December 1, 1941

Japanese military leaders make the official decision to attack Pearl Harbor

December 2, 1941

Yamamoto gives order to proceed with attack

December 7, 1941

Before 4:35 A.M.

A Japanese submarine is spotted near Pearl Harbor

6:15 A.M.

The first attack wave leaves Japanese aircraft carriers

6:30 A.M.

Japanese submarine is sunk by USS *Ward*

7:02 A.M.

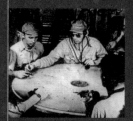

Radar operators spot a "blip" of approaching aircraft off the northern tip of Oahu

7:39 A.M.

Radar "blip" is lost in the echoes
from the surrounding mountains

7:55 A.M.

 First wave of
the Japanese
attack hits
Pearl Harbor
installations

9:55 A.M.

Japanese pilots return to their carriers

December 8, 1941

The United States declares war
on Japan

December 10, 1941

Japan invades the Philippines and takes
over Guam

December 23, 1941

Japan seizes Wake Island

January 7, 1942

Japanese attack Bataan in
the Philippines

January 27, 1942

First Japanese warship sunk by
a U.S. submarine

February 24, 1942

U.S. forces attack Japanese on
Wake Island

April 9, 1942

U.S. forces on Bataan surrender
unconditionally to the Japanese

May 5, 1942

Japanese prepare to invade Midway
and the Aleutian Islands

June 4–6, 1942

United States defeats Japan in the
Battle of Midway

June 1942

Japan takes over all of the Philippines

August 8, 1942

U.S. Marines take the unfinished airfield
on Guadalcanal

January 31, 1943

United States defeats Japan
at Guadalcanal

August 10, 1943

Guam is recaptured by U.S. forces

October 20, 1943

U.S. forces invade the Philippines

October 23–25, 1943

Japanese fleet is destroyed at the
Battle of Leyte Gulf

March 2–4, 1943

U.S. forces defeat Japan in the Battle
of Bismarck Sea

June 19, 1944

U.S. carrier-based fighter pilots shoot
down 220 Japanese planes, losing just
20 of their own planes during the
"Marianas Turkey Shoot"

Timeline

July 19, 1944

U.S. Marines invade Guam

July 27, 1944

 American troops complete the liberation of Guam

August 8, 1944

American troops capture the Mariana Islands

January 9, 1945

The U.S. Army invades Lingayen Gulf on Luzon

February 16, 1945

U.S. troops recapture Bataan

March 3, 1945

U.S. and Filipino troops capture Manila

March 16, 1945

U.S. forces capture Iwo Jima

May 20, 1945

Japanese forces begin to withdraw from China

June 20, 1945

U.S. forces capture Okinawa

June 28, 1945

The end of Japanese resistance in the Philippines is announced

June 30, 1945

U.S. forces retake the Philippines

July 5, 1945

The liberation of the Philippines is declared

August 6, 1945

The first atomic bomb is dropped on Hiroshima

August 8, 1945

The second atomic bomb is dropped on Nagasaki

August 14, 1945

Japan surrenders

Historic Sites

USS *Arizona* Memorial
1 Arizona Memorial Place
Honolulu, HI 96818
808/422-0561
Memorial spans the sunken USS *Arizona* and is a place
for quiet remembrance of those who were killed aboard.

World War II Memorial
17th Street
Washington, D.C.
202/619-7222
Honors soldiers who served in World War II
and those who supported them from home.

Look for all the books in this series

The Cuban Missile Crisis:
To the Brink of War
ISBN 0-7565-1624-2

Hiroshima and Nagasaki:
Fire from the Sky
ISBN 0-7565-1621-8

The Korean War:
America's Forgotten War
ISBN 0-7565-1625-0

Pearl Harbor:
Day of Infamy
ISBN 0-7565-1622-6

September 11:
Attack on America
ISBN 0-7565-1620-X

The Tet Offensive:
Turning Point of the Vietnam War
ISBN 0-7565-1623-4

Glossary

aircraft carrier
a ship that carries planes and helicopters and that has a runway on deck for takeoffs and landings

ally
a person or country united with another for a common purpose

ambassador
a government official who represents his or her country in a foreign country

ammunition
material that is fired from a weapon

barracks
buildings used to house soldiers

caliber
the caliber of a weapon refers to the size of its bullets in diameter

communicate
discuss or explain plans and ideas

comply
to agree to or obey someone's request

diplomat
someone who deals with other nations to create or maintain good relationships

deliberately
on purpose

dry dock
a dock where the water can be drained out so ships can be repaired

emblem
a symbol

enlist
to volunteer to serve in the military

fleet
a group of warships that operate together

hangar
a structure where aircraft are stored and repaired

immobilize
to keep something from moving or being used

implication
what something seems to mean

initiated
started

infamy
the state of being infamous, which is having an evil or detestable reputation

isolationism
a national policy to avoid involvement in the political or economic affairs of other nations

maneuver
a military movement

mooring
a place where a ship is secured, either with ropes or an anchor, to keep it from moving

navigable
able to be sailed through

offensive
attack

ordnance
military weapons, ammunition,
and maintenance equipment

periscope
a device used in a submarine that
allows the sailors inside the vessel
to see what is happening above
the water

porthole
a small windowlike hatch on a ship

recruit
new member of the armed forces

sabotage
to destroy property

seaplane ramp
a dock used to get to planes that
have floats for taking off and landing
in water

shrapnel
pieces that have broken off from an
explosive shell

stationed
positioned

suffocate
die from lack of air

tactics
actions taken to achieve a goal

torpedo
a self-propelled underwater explosive
devise

ultimately
in the end

SOURCE NOTES

Chapter 3

Page 25, line 3: Yamamoto to Shigeharu Matsumoto. 23 Nov. 2005 <http://www.rjgeib.com/heroes/tanimizu/yamamoto.html>.

Page 29, line 20: Nathan Anthony and Robert Gardner. *The Bombing of Pearl Harbor in American History.* Berkeley Heights, N.J.: Enslow Publishers, 2001, p. 22.

Chapter 4

Page 31, line 9: William E. Shapiro. *Turning Points of World War II: Pearl Harbor.* New York: Franklin Watts, 1984, p. 40.

Page 33, line 8: November 27 dispatch by CNO to CincPac and CincAF, p. 30. Department of the Navy. 23 Nov. 2005 <http://www.ibiblio.org/pha/pha/narrative/27.html>.

Page 35, line 2: Pearl Harbor Timeline. 23 Nov. 2005 <http://plasma.nationalgeographic.com/pearlharbor/history/pearlharbor_timeline.html>.

Chapter 5

Page 45, line 7: Thomas B. Allen. *Remember Pearl Harbor: American and Japanese Survivors Tell Their Stories.* Washington, D.C.: National Geographic, 2001, p. 25.

Chapter 6

Page 48, line 8: *The Bombing of Pearl Harbor in American History*, p. 30.

Chapter 8

Page 76, line 6: Interview with Stephen B. Young. *Pearl Harbor* Special Edition DVD. Walt Disney Home Video, 2003.

Chapter 9

Page 83, line 5: Winston Churchill. *Memoirs of the Second World War.* New York: Houghton Mifflin Books, 1991, p.506.

Page 83–86, line 20: Archives. Hyde Park, New York: Franklin Delano Roosevelt Library. 23 Nov. 2005 <http://www.fdrlibrary.marist.edu/oddec7.html>.

SELECT BIBLIOGRAPHY

Harris, Nathaniel. *Pearl Harbor.* North Pomfret, Vt.: David and Charles, 1986.

Hopkinson, Deborah. *Pearl Harbor.* New York: Dillon Press, 1991.

Krensky, Stephen. *Pearl Harbor.* New York: Simon and Schuster, 2001.

Rosenberg, Emily. *A Date Which Will Live: Pearl Harbor in American Memory.* Durham, N.C.: Duke University Press, 2003.

Tanaka, Shelley. *Attack on Pearl Harbor: The True Story of the Day America Entered World War II.* New York: Hyperion Books for Children, 2001.

Wels, Susan. *Pearl Harbor: December 7, 1941: America's Darkest Day.* San Diego: Tehabi Books, 2001.

FURTHER READING

Allen, Thomas B. *Remember Pearl Harbor: American and Japanese Survivors Tell Their Stories.* Washington, D.C.: National Geographic Society, 2001.

Anthony, Nathan, and Robert Gardner. *The Bombing of Pearl Harbor in American History.* Berkeley Heights, N.J.: Enslow Publishers, 2001.

McGowen, Tom. *The Attack on Pearl Harbor.* New York: Children's Press, 2002.

Tames, Richard. *Pearl Harbor: The U.S. Enters World War II.* Chicago: Heinemann Library, 2001.

Index

ABOUT THE AUTHOR

Stephanie Fitzgerald has been writing nonfiction for children for more than 10 years. Her specialties include history, wildlife, and popular culture. Stephanie's grandfather, August Berardinelli ("Poppy Augie"), was one of the thousands of young men who joined the Navy after the attack on Pearl Harbor.

IMAGE CREDITS